Bonsai Tree Care

A Practical Beginners Guide To Bonsai Gardening

Copyright 2015 by Better Life Solutions- All rights reserved.

This document is geared towards providing exact and reliable information in regards to the topic and issue covered. The publication is sold with the idea that the publisher is not required to render accounting, officially permitted, or otherwise, qualified services. If advice is necessary, legal or professional, a practiced individual in the profession should be ordered.

- From a Declaration of Principles which was accepted and approved equally by a Committee of the American Bar Association and a Committee of Publishers and Associations.

In no way is it legal to reproduce, duplicate, or transmit any part of this document in either electronic means or in printed format. Recording of this publication is strictly prohibited and any storage of this document is not allowed unless with written permission from the publisher. All rights reserved.

The information provided herein is stated to be truthful and consistent, in that any liability, in terms of inattention or otherwise, by any usage or abuse of any policies, processes, or directions contained within is the solitary and utter responsibility of the recipient reader. Under no circumstances will any legal responsibility or blame be held against the publisher for any reparation, damages, or monetary loss due to the information herein, either directly or indirectly.

Respective authors own all copyrights not held by the publisher.

The information herein is offered for informational purposes solely, and is universal as so. The presentation of the information is without contract or any type of guarantee assurance.

The trademarks that are used are without any consent, and the publication of the trademark is without permission or backing by the trademark owner. All trademarks and brands within this book are for clarifying purposes only and are the owned by the owners themselves, not affiliated with this document.

Table of Contents

Introduction 4

Chapter 1 - What is Bonsai? 5

Chapter 2 - The Best Examples of Bonsai 17

Chapter 3 - Choosing the Right Bonsai for You 21

Chapter 4 - How to Grow Bonsai? 26

Chapter 5 - New Plant 35

Introduction

This book contains proven steps and strategies on how to grow bonsai trees, but also to find out which type of tree suits your personality the best. You can also read about the history of this art and check out some of the finest examples of bonsai trees.

Here Is A Preview Of What You'll Learn...

- What is a bonsai
- History of bonsai, from ancient times to the modern day
- Most beautiful examples of bonsai trees in the world
- How to choose the right tree for you
- The easiest ways to grow a bonsai tree

Much, much more!

Chapter 1 - What is Bonsai?

An ancient Japanese quote says that Bonsai trees represent harmony in nature - contained. It is perfect for anybody who appreciates their understated beauty and unique form. A bonsai tree is a symbol of harmony. The growing of bonsai trees combines will, determination, honor and patience, which result in satisfaction and happiness.

Bonsai, the ancient Japanese art of growing trees in a pot, is truly a magnificent blend of art, skills and determination. The thousand-year tradition of bonsai trees, which in Europe became known at the beginning of the 20th century, continues to be in considered an almost mystical art. With a good reason.

A fascinating fusion of sculpture and horticulture produces miniature trees which many consider art. It is a fact that there are some centuries-old specimens of bonsai, which are of a great interest to rich people, thus having astronomical prices. Of course, such examples are rare.

What is needed to deal with bonsai? In fact, growing bonsai trees is a quite simple hobby, but it demands patience, love and commitment. If you are interested in this unique way of growing trees, lots of quality literature can be found on the internet and the basics are explained in this book. If you are a beginner, it is not necessary to buy a set of tools, just get the most basic ones that you can find in most shopping centers.

Bonsai can be held anywhere: on the window, on the balcony, on the porch, in the yard, in the garden. The only place where bonsai cannot keep is in a closed room. Bonsai must always be in the open air, while in an enclosed space, it can endure a maximum of 2-3 days.

Great attention should be paid when selecting the pot, because the beauty of bonsai in whole, comes from both the plant and the container. The pot should emphasize the beauty of wood and not distract the eye of the viewer. They are mostly made of ceramic or wood, neutral color and flat and shallow design. This doesn't apply to a cascading form of trees when tall and narrow pots are required.

As far as tools for dealing with bonsai, they are easily available and are inexpensive. The tools can be purchased at each center for the construction and home decoration. Pliers, small rake and wires are essential tools for growing and maintaining bonsai. The branches are trimmed with scissors and stringings, in order to make the desired shape. If you purchase a plant which correspond to the conditions you have, the maintenance is simple: regular watering (usually more often for outdoor than indoor plants), fertilizing (fertilizer which corresponds to large specimens of the same species), and occasionally cropping.

People grow plants in pots for thousands of years (spices, herbs, and plants for decoration), because of the beauty of a flower or leaf. But in China, at the time of the Han Dynasty (about A.D. 200 BC), monks created a new concept - the creation of miniature natural landscapes in containers, called Penjing. One of the many legends tells how the emperor felt lengthy trips to the countryside boring, so he ordered the miniature replicas of his empire built in the courtyard of the palace, facing the bedroom window, which he could see his entire estate. Wanting to preserve its uniqueness, he ordered that if someone else tries to do something like that, should be killed as a traitor. Whether true or not, one thing is certain, owning a miniature landscape was a status symbol.

The oldest written document about bonsai was found in the tomb of Prince Zhang Huai, who died in 706. Two wall paintings in the tomb show servants carrying a miniature landscape with rocks and plants in the pot of lotus shape. A version of bonsai, called penjing was greatly appreciated during the Song Dynasty (960 - 1279 AD), during which it developed into a more sophisticated art form. Then begins the cultivation of bonsai as we know it today - a single tree in a bonsai pot. These first examples had the pots carved to resemble dragons and other animals.

Throughout the 11th and 12th century, China has carried out a significant cultural impact on neighboring countries, particularly Japan, through art and philosophy. For transmission of bonsai in Japan and spread among the Japanese aristocracy, the Samurai, the most deserving were Zen monks. For them, the bonsai was a religious facility "green stairs to the sky", or the link between people and God. In the center of growing bonsai trees is the balance between man and nature. The cultivation requires a lot of care and attention, but as a reward brings calmness of mind, a sense of refreshment and inner peace.

It was not until the Muromachi era in the 14th century that bonsai became popular. Together with origami, ikebana, Suiseki and tea ceremony (Chado), bonsai became a part of Japanese culture. In the 18th century, Bonsai art reached its peak and was extremely appreciated. Some techniques of bonsai growing started being ritualized during that period. From Japan, bonsai spread to the West in the late 19th century. Bonsai exhibitions were held in Paris in 1878, 1889, 1900, while the first major one was held in London in 1909. Unlike in the past, today, bonsai is not only a privilege of the upper class. It turned into a renowned and horticultural art worldwide.

Bonsai is a Japanese art form which uses small trees that are grown in pots. "Bonsai" is a Japanese word, which comes from the earlier Chinese term - penzai. "Bon" is a tray pot which is used in bonsai culture. The word bonsai is often used in English as an umbrella term that covers all miniature trees in containers or pots. There are similar practices to bonsai that exist in other cultures, particularly in the Chinese tradition of Penjin, as well as in some cultural traditions of Vietnam. Japanese tradition is over a millennia old and has its own rules and terminology. "Bonsai" is a Japanese word, which comes from the earlier Chinese term - penzai. "Bon" is a tray pot which is used in bonsai culture. The word bonsai is often used in English as an umbrella term that covers all miniature trees in containers or pots.

Bonsai is a copy of the original species, in a much smaller dimension. This may be done with cutting, seedling, or with other techniques for handling small trees. Bonsai can be created from almost any tree with true branches, which means it can be cultivated to remain small. This can be achieved through container confinement with crown and root pruning. Some species are popular as bonsai trees because they have certain characteristics, which allow them to look like a big tree, only much, much smaller. These attributes include small leaves and needles.

The purpose of bonsai is to allow the viewer to enjoy contemplation and the satisfaction for the grower while growing the tree. In contrast to other plant cultivation practices, bonsai is not used as a for food, nor as a medicine. Bonsai is also not suitable for creating landscapes. Actually, bonsai practice set focus only on the cultivation and shaping the small for the purpose of enjoying their existence.

In order to call a tree a bonsai, it needs to follow certain patterns and to meet the aesthetic standards of bonsai. When bonsai tree reaches the planned size, it is planted in a pot screen, usually one designed for bonsai display in one of the few accepted shapes and proportions. From that moment on, its growth is limited to the pot. Throughout the years, the bonsai is shaped in order to limit growth and meet the artists detailed design.

Do not confuse the practice of bonsai with dwarfing, which people sometimes do. Dwarfing generally refers to research and creation of genetically mutated plants that are miniatures of existing species. Bonsai instead depends on growing small trees from regular stock and seeds. Bonsai uses cultivation techniques like pruning, root reduction, watering, defoliation and vaccination to produce small trees that mimic the shape and style of mature, large trees.

Japanese art of bonsai originated from the Chinese practice of Penjing. As Japanese people started becoming close to Chinese in the early Middle Ages, they started appreciating their culture. Buddhist students from Japan who were visiting and returning from China, started bringing back Chinese cultural practices, including bonsai. The Imperial diplomats first saw bonsai as a thing of prestige. Artifacts found in Japan that are dating back to the 7th century, include examples of miniature trees. Bonsai from this period consists of a wooden tray on which sides mountains and river banks are depicted.

In the Middle Ages, bonsai trees were considered to be a sign of prestige among those people from the upper class. Although, bonsai trees were mostly produced in China, they were very popular in Japan. Imported from China, bonsai kept in Japanese homes showed the owner's wealth and exquisite cultural upbringing. Chinese Chan Buddhist monks came to teach in monasteries in Japan during the Millde Ages. Among the things they introduced to Japan is the art of making miniature plants. Japanese political leaders of the day saw it as an ideal pastime for men of taste.

In the early 14th century, a famous Chinese priest and poet, Kokan Shiren wrote down the foundations of bonsai art. It quickly became very popular in Japan, where his work was considered the manual of bonsai growing.Since then, many influential Japanese people started writing publications on their own, each giving a personal touch to the bonsai culture.

Kyuzo Murat (1902-1991) was one of the few people who took care of bonsai during the Pacific War. He collected and preserved many trees from many manufacturers. During 1945, many old trees were the smallest victims of the spring and summer bombing of Tokyo and sixty-six other cities. Gardeners of the Imperial Palace protected trees by pouring water on them, after the palace caught fire when neighboring areas were bombarded. After the surrender of Japan, a re-evaluation of the war began and the recovery of damaged collections of trees, including the imperial bonsai trees lasted more than a decade. During the Allied occupation of Japan (to 1952), US officials and their wives have taken courses in bonsai, bonkei, ikebana, and other traditional arts and crafts, as provided by General MacArthur's staff.

After the World War II, the number of trends have affected the Japanese bonsai tradition. One of the key trends was the increase in the number, scope and prominence of bonsai exhibition. For example, ten bonsai displays appeared only in 1947, after the break of four years, and became annual happenings. In October 1964 the Great Exhibition was held in Hibya Park, which gave bonsai art a major international recognition. Other countries began presenting exhibitions of bonsai as well, repeating events now started taking place in Taiwan and many other places in Asia, Australia, the United States, and several European countries, among others.

Another key was the increase in quantity of books on the subject and related arts. The first formal bonsai courses open to the public and foreigners in Tokyo. Koehn was a fan before the war, and his 1937 book Japanese Tray Landscapes published in English in Beijing.

The third trend was the growing availability of bonsai experts who provided training for future growers. Initially this was happening only in Japan, but then spread beyond. Back in the US, these people formed the American Bonsai

Society. Other groups and individuals outside of Asia then visited and studied in various Japanese schools, sometimes even as a trainee under teachers. These visitors returned to their local clubs, the latest techniques and styles, which can then spread further. Japanese teachers traveled around the globe.

The final trend supports the global participation in bonsai art by expanding the availability of bonsai soil materials, specialty papers, tools, containers, and other items. Bonsai grows in Japan announced that they would ship bonsai trees worldwide. Most countries now have local nurseries that provide plant growth. Japanese bonsai soil components such as clay are available worldwide, while local providers also provide similar materials in many places.

Bonsai has now definitely reached a worldwide audience. There are more than 1,200 books on bonsai and related arts in at least twenty languages available in over ninety countries and territories. A few dozen magazines in over thirteen languages are published regularly. The internet is a great source for getting the information on everything regarding bonsai, while in this book you can find a beginner's instruction for growing a bonsai tree.

Chapter 2 - The Best Examples of Bonsai

The 800-years-old bonsai tree in Shunkai is significant not only for its very advanced age, but also for the way it was grown. Master Kobayashi, one of the most popular bonsai artists in the world, is the owner of Shunkai bonsai grove in Tokyo, which is famous for lots of high-quality trees. Nowadays, this tree is one of the most expensive bonsai trees in the world.

Bonsai tree called Goshin "protective spirits" by John Naka. Goshin translates directly as "protective spirits" for a reason. This tree has developed with a lot of spirituality involved by John Y. Naka, who started growing it in 1948. In 1984, he donated it to the National Bonsai Fondation and the tree has since been a part of the National Arboretum of the United States.

Bonsai tree owned by Morten Shohin Albek is only 9.5 cm (4 inches) high and stands on a rock in a nutshell. It is one of the most famous examples of bonsai, because of the tree beauty and a great design of the pot as well.

Bonsai Pinus silvestris. This tree is very realistic and is of a great value for bonsai trees. The pellets have a very dense foliage, as if it were clouds in the sky. Because of this, this bonsai tree belongs to most expensive trees in the world.

Chinese Penjing landscape Manlung. This beautiful Chinese landscape belongs to a collection in Hong Kong. In this landscape, trees, rocks, and miniature figures are set in a shallow rectangular container made of marble, which in turn is displayed on an antique table.

Flowering Bonsai of Wolfgang Putz. This tree is of Azalea species of only 14 cm (5 inches) height. The tree blooms short, but very lively, which is the time when most photographs of this tree are taken. The tree is planted in a Chinese pot of a great artistic importance.

Brazilian rain tree by Budi Sulistyo. This tree grows from a small pot, very detail decorated. A native of South America, this Central Brazilian rain tree is considered one of the most beautiful tropical world and one of the most popular bonsai subjects. Because of that, the tree owned by Budi Sulistyo is among the most-praised bonsai trees.

Japanese maple (Acer palmatum) of Walter Pall is apart of one of the most famous bonsai collections, which belongs to the European Bonsai artist called Walter Pall. This tree is very thin and realistic. Maple is a large (almost a meter high, which is the maximum for a tree to be called a Bonsai tree) and more than a hundred years old.

The bonsai tree of Masahiko Kimura Sensei belongs to a diverse collection of bonsai trees. Kimura started growing bonsai at the age of 15. Kimura was a pupil of master Hamano in Omiya Bonsai Village. In his fascinating and sometimes unconventional work, he developed many styles and techniques, which results are seen in this collection.

Take a look at some of these bonsai trees as it can help you along to decide if growing bonsai trees is the right hobby for you. If you fall in love with these trees, every case is that you will adore creating one bonsai art of work, on your own.

Chapter 3 - Choosing the Right Bonsai for You

Select the appropriate tree species for your climate. Depending on the species, bonsai trees can differ significantly. Many woody perennials, and even more tropical plants, can be grown in order to become bonsai trees. However, not all types are suitable for one place. When choosing the type it is important to take into account the climate in which tree will be grown. For example, some trees will be ruined in the cold weather, while others actually require temperatures to fall below zero, so that they can enter into sleep mode and prepare for spring. Before you start growing your bonsai tree, you need to make sure that the type you choose can survive in the area, in which you live. This especially goes, if you plan on having the tree outdoors. Staff at the local garden store can help if you are unsure.

The various juniper bonsai tree are perfect choices for beginners. These evergreen trees are survivors. They can endure in most of the areas in the northern hemisphere, while even the more temperate regions of the southern hemisphere can suit them. In addition, the spruce trees grow easily - they respond well to pruning and other efforts. Because they are evergreen trees, these species will never lose their leaves and if they do, you will know that something is wrong.

Other species that are mostly grown as bonsai trees are pine, fir and cedar trees of many varieties. Leafy trees are another option - Japanese maples are particularly beautiful, such as magnolias, oaks, and elms. Finally, some that are woody tropical plants, such as jade and snowrose are a good option for indoors, in cold or temperate climates.

Decide if you are planning on having a tree indoors or outdoors. The needs of bonsai indoors and outdoors can differ a lot. In general, the internal environment is dryer and receive less light than the open air environment, so you will want to choose a tree with corresponding light conditions and humidity. Here are some of the most common types of bonsai trees, grouped by their suitability for either internal or external environment are listed below:

Inside: Ficus, Gardenia, Camellia, Kingsville boxwood, Hawaiian umbrella, Serissa, etc.

External: juniper, birch, beech, cypress, cedar, maple, ginkgo, larch, elm, etc.

Keep in mind that some of the hardier varieties such as juniper are suitable for use indoors and outdoors, providing that they are properly cared for.

Choose the size of your bonsai. Bonsai trees come in many sizes. Grown trees can be as small as 6 inches (15.2 cm) high and large 3 feet (0.9 m) in height, depending on the type. If you decide to grow your bonsai trees from seed or a court of another tree, that can start even smaller. You will need to make sure you have more more water, much more soil and slightly more sunlight, if you decide on a larger bonsai tree instead of a small one.

Just a few things you will want to consider when deciding on the size of your bonsai tree:

- Container size
- Available space in your home or office

- The availability of sunlight in your home or office

- The amount of care that you will be able to put in your bonsai tree (remember that larger trees take longer to prune)

Choose a pot. A special feature is that the bonsai trees planted in pots that limit their growth. Most important is to decide which pot to use. You must ensure that the pot is large enough to provide enough land for covering the whole root of a plant. When you water your trees, they will absorb moisture from the soil through its roots. But, you do not want to have a small amount of soil in the pot so that the roots of the trees cannot retain moisture.

In order to prevent the root rotting, you want to make sure that your pot has one or more drainage holes in the bottom. If it doesn't have them already, you can drill the holes yourself.

While the pot should be of the size that will be suitable for a large tree, you also want to maintain a clean, neat aesthetics of your bonsai tree. Too large pots can make the tree look very small, making an unusual or mismatched look. Buying a pot large enough so that the roots of the tree fit. It must not be much more - the idea is to complement the pot with the tree aesthetically, but at the same time, in a relatively unobtrusive way. Some prefer to grow their bonsai in ordinary, practical containers, while then transferring them to nicer containers when they are fully grown. This process is especially useful if your type of bonsai trees is a fragile one, allowing you to defer the purchase of "good" pot until you make sure the tree is doing alright.

Chapter 4 - How to Grow Bonsai?

What is needed to deal with bonsai? Any person interested in bonsai first asks: "What we all need to deal with bonsai? How much is growing a bonsai a demanding hobby? "The short answer is:" Bonsai requires more attention than the jars with flowers, but not even close regarding the time or finances as pets such dogs or cats do." The basic conditions for dealing with bonsai are:

Adequate space. A window in which the flat pots with flowers and trees is a minimum needed for growing bonsai trees. Anything larger than that is excellent.

Time for watering - ten minutes (or less) a day and a friend to have the trees watered when you are away.

A bit of money - especially for the tree (although the tree and we can extract from nature), then the container, substrate, fertilizer, some tools and wire.

Growing flowers and ornamental plants is a common occurrence, among the people all over the world. The practice of bonsai is, however, a quite rare hobby beyond Japan and many consider bonsai a mystical concept. One of the many questions that people who first come into contact with bonsai ask is: What do I need, what conditions do I need if I want to keep bonsai? Bonsai often seems complicated hobby. On the contrary! Bonsai is essentially quite simple hobby, and the requirements needed to get started in this hobby are presented in the next few chapters.

Space. The basic prerequisite for holding bonsai is, of course, that you have a place where you will keep it. Bonsai can be held anywhere: on the window, on the balcony, on the porch, in the yard, in the garden. The only place where bonsai cannot keep it - in a closed room. Bonsai must always be in the fresh air. In an enclosed space, it can enter a maximum of 2-3 days. The air in the room occupied with people is suitable for some species of subtropical and tropical plants, but in most cases bonsai usually belongs to those species to whom air in the room does not fit. Therefore, the main precondition for holding bonsai is open space. It is appropriate to set some form of a balcony or window in which you hold pots with flowers.

Bonsai trees need to be relatively often watered. The biggest heat is prevailing during the summer holidays, when we go on vacation, and during that period bonsai needs watering every day. A similar situation is with many plants that we have in the flat, when we go on a holiday. Therefore, one of the prerequisites for holding bonsai is to have it watered while you're gone. This could be your neighbor or a friend who lives nearby and is ready every day to get to your apartment and water the tree. Or you simply move their trees at a friend or relatives who will water them, while you're gone. Changing the environment will not harm them as long as they are regularly irrigated and kept outdoors.

This problem is expressed only through the summer holidays. In winter, when there is snow, trees do not need watering. Therefore, to skiing, you can go without ensuring there is a person to make your tree watered. Same goes for most of the spring and autumn periods of the year, but not during summer, unless you live in very cold climate.

As already hinted in the previous paragraph, the trees, except in winter, need to be relatively often watered, which requires a certain amount of time. If you only have one tree, then it is less than a minute a day. If you have a dozen or more bonsai, watering time does not exceed ten to fifteen minutes.

How often the trees are in the need for watering? It depends on the season and weather conditions. Bonsai trees are not watered according to a strict rule. Instead, you should simply pay attention to the trees, monitor soil moisture and water if required. However, for the purposes of this book, we will slightly simplify things in order to get a general picture of how many hours are needed for watering.

During the winter, while the trees are resting, they require almost no watering. If temperatures are above zero, it is necessary to water the tree every week or two. If the substrate is frozen or if the trees snowing, then it does not need watering until the snow melts.

The period in which the trees grow up, depends from species to species and from region to region, but coincides roughly with the spring, summer and autumn. At the beginning and the end of the growing season, trees need watering every 3-4 days, and when the trees are in full growth trees, they should be watered every day or two. During extreme heat, the trees need watering every day. It is also the most difficult period when it comes to watering, as was mentioned earlier.

Maintenance. Besides watering trees, the plants are needed to be maintained. During the growing season is necessary for every tree to be cropped approximately every 2 weeks. Trees' fastest growing period is the spring and early summer, while later, their growth slows, so pruning is not as often. For one, pruning trees need between 10 minutes and half an hour, depending on the type and size of the plant.

Once a year the tree should be transplanted or shaped. Only one of these two things should be done as a tree cannot stand to be both transplanted and shaped in the same year. Although, sometimes nothing bad will happen to the tree, it is better to choose only one of these two things. Designing the tree, the so called tree-styling, should be performed once every year (except in those years when transplanted) and it lasts about an hour or two for simpler trees, up to 5-6 hours for extremely complicated bonsai trees.

Tree. In order to deal with a bonsai art, we need, of course, a tree. Bonsai is not a special kind of tree as it is pine or hornbeam or beech. Bonsai can be grown from various types of tree. Trees that are sold by a variety of shopping malls as "bonsai" are not suitable material for any serious dealing with bonsai. Trees from which we make bonsai we can get in two ways: buy them in the nursery or take them in nature. Whichever way we decide we need the money.

Prices of the trees from the bonsai grove range from a couple of dollars to several thousand dollars (if you buy a tree of the world class). But for the beginner's level, you should not spend too much money. If the tree is attained from nature, the tree does not cost us anything, but we need to buy some digging tools.

In case you're pulling wood from nature, we need a container and substrate. If you buy a tree in the nursery, you'll transplant it in a year, so we also need pots and substrate. The first 2-3 years, tree should be placed in an ordinary plastic container for flowers that can be purchased at most groves or shopping centers. Receptacles after 2-3 years put finished bonsai (so-called. "Bonsai pots") are significantly more expensive, but they give you and so will not be necessary for the initial phase. The substrate in which we put bonsai is also an extensive topic that deserves a series of articles, but in short, a larger substrate package is sufficient for planting and replanting approximately 3 large or 10 small wood.

Due to the nature of the substrate in which it is necessary to put wood, it frequently needs to be recharged (fertilization). Supplemental feeding begins in the early growing season (March) and lasts throughout the season until the beginning of dormancy (October) . Feeding performed at regular intervals should be done approximately once a week.

To deal with bonsai, one requires several tools. Luckily, it is enough to start with the tools that most households already have: Backhoe, electrical wire cutters, Swiss Army knife, sharp scissors. These tools are not adapted to work in the bonsai and for a serious engagement is necessary to buy a specialized tool. Therefore bonsai enthusiast first start to work with the tools for other purposes which they already own, and slowly, each year, buy one or two pieces of specialized bonsai tools. Getting scissors can wait a year from the beginning of dealing with bonsai.

Designing bonsai trees is almost unthinkable without the use of "bonsai wire". Two types of wire are used - aluminum wire and tempered copper wire, so the next item in the list should be wires. Both types of wire can be purchased at the hardware store and purchasing stations of secondary raw materials. In addition to the wire type, it is essential to think about the thickness (diameter). The thickness of the branches depends on the thickness of the wire that we use. The wire can be also purchased online or at retailers bonsai equipment.

In addition to the above-mentioned costs, there are costs that every hobby carries: the purchase of books, courses, workshops, trips to exhibitions and the like. However, bonsai can be addressed without it. However, experience shows that once a person falls in love with bonsai, travel to the other end of the world to see the exhibition of small trees has become a normal occurrence.

Bonsai is a living thing that grows with you. One of the most important things that is needed to deal with bonsai is love of small trees. Once you get your first tree, very soon you will be sure that the bonsai hobby is the right for you, or not. Because the plant requires us to love it and care. It needs to be watered almost every day, it is necessary to monitor its growth, taking care that it is sufficiently fed and that it does not get attacked by a parasite or disease. But, the tree will give back love to you, in the form of the beautiful scenery on your balcony or in your garden. And that's just the beginning. Once you enter the world of bonsai, you will hardly be able to easily get out of it.

Chapter 5 - New Plant

The plant will have more branches and stems that do not contribute to the design you are looking for. Remove any branches that will not help you on your way. Want a strong form of the trunk? By removing all the small branches around the base you can achieve that. The trunk branches should be run from the bottom to the top of the plant. The plant should begin to resemble a small tree for now. Branches that have chosen to take their design should be reduced if they are too big and out of proportion with the rest of the plant. Select side plants that will be in front of your pot and work on the other side now. This has to be the best part of the plant.

The first branch of the plant should be a one third of the way up the trunk of the plant. This is how a tree forms in nature. From there, remove branches that do not contribute to the balance of the branches of trees and wires, to fill the gaps where there should be no branches at all. The tops of the trees must form a triangle. The top of the tree is the highest point and with the lowest lows that come at the end, makes a triangle. Older trees have a horizontal branching or even slightly tilted to the downside.

Check the plant to make sure it is dry. That will change with the season and the maturity of the plant in its pot. Water the plants thoroughly, so that the water runs out the drainage holes. It is also better for foliage plants to clean the leaves of the tree. Do not spray the leaves in direct sunlight or at night. Most plants need a partial light and cannot cope with direct sunlight. Be careful where to place the bonsai tree in the house. The window to the east with morning sun is the best environment.

Repot the plant in early spring, in the time before the plant shows signs of growth. Remove excess soil from the roots and cut off all the roots that are thicker than a pencil, promoting smaller feeder roots. This decreases the likelihood of surrounding the roots. Cut all the root ball and return to its original container with fresh soil. Smaller plants should be repotted every two to three years. A mixture of soil should contain equal parts of sand, peat and perlite.

Winter Care

During the winter, the temperatures on the Nort Hemisphere can be very low, which in turn, can be very harmful to your bonsai tree. Because of that, most of the bonsai groves are selling indoor plants which can and should stay at home all the time, regardless of the time of the year. There are plants such as maples and evergreens that are outdoor plants and should be put in a room if the temperatures drop extremely. Heating garage is a good place to plant your bonsai tree, or you can bury their pots, mulch, and cover with a cone to keep the roots from freezing and killing the plant. When the weather warms in spring, gradually bring plants and expose to moderate amounts of sunlight at the same time, each day.

Bonsai Tools and Programs

Scissors are the number one tool when it comes to bonsai tee growing. You need scissors that allow you to do a good deed of the cutting in a small space. These scissors should be strong and should only be used for bonsai work. You may want to buy a little bit more expensive scissors, even if you are a beginner. Over time, you'll want shears specially made for bonsai work.

Concave cutters. Although this tool is not as widespread as regular scissors, for example, this is probably the most important piece of equipment you can buy. Concave cutters can cut the branches of trees and leave behind a concave wound. The wound heals more rapidly than the straight cut. Because of that, this type of cutters is an essential part of your bonsai tool collection.

Wire. Although you will not immediately need a wire, it is wise to get it as soon as you start growing bonsai trees. You will need to get a couple of different thickness. It is very flexible until it bends, then establishes and maintains its position. You will use it to set the position of the branches and stations.

Key cutters. These are very similar concave cutters above, except that the spherical head allows you to cut the branches and leave a little concave scar. This is very useful, but not as important as a good set of concave cutters.

Folding saw. It is a useful tool to cut through the diameter of either concave or branches. This is especially important when working with large trees.

Although tools are very important for growing bonsai trees, they are not as important as your determination. If you want to grow a bonsai tree, you need to be prepared to spend a lot of time and invest love in your project. In return, bonsai tree will give you the satisfaction of doing a great work.

Finally, if you enjoyed this book, then I'd like to ask you for a favor, would you be kind enough to leave a review for this book on Amazon? It'd be greatly appreciated!

Thank you and good luck!

Printed in Great Britain
by Amazon